Hi! Have a Nice Day

First published in Great Britain 1972
© 1972 by Fortress Press

Printed in Great Britain
by Wood Westworth & Co. Ltd., St. Helens, Lancashire

Open 6

Fresh Thoughts

from

Fresh Kids

who say:

Hi!

Have a Nice Day

by

NORMAN C. HABEL

Photographs

by

BRUCE MISFELDT

LUTTERWORTH PRESS
GUILDFORD AND LONDON

THE NICE DAYS BEHIND "HI"

All kids are creative. There's a kid in every kid! There's a soaring eagle in everyone. But one day someone says, "Don't paint over the lines, Mary." And Mary is squashed. Her eagle never leaves the rocks. Her feeling of exploration is gradually curbed. "Girls don't play in the mud." "Girls don't climb trees." "Girls don't fly like eagles." "Girls play with dolls." That's the party line. But there's no party, no straining of the imagination. And somehow the church is partly to blame. Pews are not good news for creative kids. Yet the church can be the very arena where new things can happen. That's where it should be possible to accept people no matter what they make or make up. The church is the place for dreams, wild ideas, hopes, clashing colors, nonsense, and celebration. For we trust a Lord who rose from the dead to laugh in the face of every set of lines that forces people into phony squares. He frees us to paint. He frees us to cross the lines. And he frees us to stay in the lines if that is best for our friend's painting. There's a new Adam or Eve inside each of us. Christ created him/her through our baptism and his power. He created him/her to create. Our task is to arouse that new person within. It's time to free our imaginations, our faith, our laughter, our hopes. It's time to reach deep into ourselves and find the new person within, who is the true person God has made us to be. Find that person and say, Hi. Have a nice day.

Over the past few years I have attended many youth gatherings, celebrations, workshops, and happenings. I've been searching for the new man and the new woman in youth. And I've found them many times. The morsels of feeling, faith, satire, laughter, prayer, and folly collected in this book are examples of new people at work. They express moments of new creation, agony, and celebration. They are the combined birth of kids, kids with me, and me with kids.

HAVE A NICE DAY WITH "HI"

This book is a mixed bag of morsels . . . a grab bag! But there should be something here to your taste . . . something to tickle your imagination, quicken your senses, lift your worship. These are baskets of bread and grass left from the feeding of the five thousand in many fields and towns. These are fragments from youth gatherings that can grow into new loaves and lives at other youth gatherings or workshops or services. They are for fun, feeling, and folly. They are for having a nice day. They say, Hi! In short, there are three bags full:

1. **HI, HAVE A NICE DAY.** The first pieces ask you to imagine you have just been born or reborn. Your senses are as sharp as singing silence. Your world is a new creation to be explored. Your day is a new day, the first day, a birthday. Breath, water, baptism, sunshine, and love are as fresh as the morning. Everything is new and touchable. Find the pieces that touch you. And you may discover fragments of faith that will help you open the feelings of others. These pieces are for openers.

2. **HI, HAVE A GOOD FRIDAY.** The battle of Calvary is not over. Death is still imposed upon living people in our world. And we hear the muffled cry of people for whom almost every Friday is a Good Friday. So the pieces of this basket are echoes of the seven words from the cross. They are seven words of pain that cut us to the quick in our own society. They are words followed by pleas that you may like to use for Lent, for a Good Friday service (where they began), or when you feel the pain within. And I hope you do . . . that your Friday may indeed be God's . . . and Good.

3. **HI, HAVE A PURPLE LEMON.** If "birth" characterizes Part One and "death" Part Two, I suppose "resurrection" is the power of Part Three. Here satire, laughter, liturgy, celebration, and drama combine to provide the possibility for a festival of new life, a carnival of joy before the empty tomb. Imagination breaks through the surface to say a fierce YES to life in the face of death and a fantastic HI in the face of every ugly foe.

CONTENTS

1 Hi! Have a Nice Day

2 Hi Have a Good Friday

3 Hi! Have a Purple Lemon

1

Hi!
Have a Nice Day

MY MORNING CRY
(*before I wake*)

Hi God!

Prod me with the odd!
Dazzle me with today!
And catch me a dragon!
OK? OK!

TALK WITH ME
(*beneath the storm*)

Could you take off a day
and talk with me?

I have my life on my mind
like a stray dog in the woods
who has just found
a turtle.

Could you take off a day
and stray
with me
where
turtles talk?

MY EVENING CRY
(before I scream)

Lord,
the edges of my mind
and the shape of my world
are as fuzzy as the night mist.

I'm not sure where I am, often,
where I am going,
why I think the thoughts I do
and whether it's worth
searching for something.

It's like being in a daze
without any sense of direction
or clear road ahead.

It's like wrestling with the sand
. . .in an endless desert.

Is there some old angel in the woods
who can grab me by the throat,
and twist my wandering mind
until I feel the real,
taste the true,
wonder at the world
and get a glimpse
of where to go tomorrow?

Would you take me on, Lord,
show me the nerves of nature
and shock me into my senses
until I feel the way?
Or will you just shine on trees
and forget about me?

Well, I won't let you go
until you bless me,
bless me with the instinct of a bird
who knows who he is
and which way to fly
when it is winter.

I won't let you go,
I won't!

NERVE ENDS

May I invite you to walk through today in search of the soft. Touch it gently with your fingers. Taste it slowly with your feelings.

May I?

Amid the grating of cogs and the grinding of bumpers, May I?

In the corners of your morning touch the tender where life is still alive. Kiss the eyelids of a child. Watch the fingertips of a gentle Man mixing soft soil and saliva to heal open the crusted eyes of a blind man.

Search for the soft where the nerve ends of the soul come to the surface. Look for a tender throb of an old man's tears or a sleeping cocoon. Feel a live fur and be fascinated.

Is it too hard to come home and search for the soft within? Can we open ourselves to sense the souls of others? Or will we wander through the evening intent on closing our core from the life beat at our side?

Deep at the center of all that is soft, love survives. For deep love is a patient pain. It absorbs the thorns until the anger is spent and a new word is born that two people remember forever.

And he who is Love, loves at the core of all love. His heart never breaks, but gives and gives and gives until we give.

As you hit the pavement this morning, may I invite you to remember your own wounds and search for the soft under His sky.

THE TASTE OF CLAY

(in Adam's mouth)
Lord,
let me be like Adam, today,
with the fingerprints of God
still fresh in my flesh.

Let me awake
to this space called world
with a wonder that cries:
Heh, I am!
I AM.

I'm not, NOT.
I AM.

Let me see
what it's like to BE.
Let me feel my birth
with the greeting of God
still ringing in the clay:
Hi, Adam, Hi!
Hi, Eve, Hi!
Have a nice day!

HAVE A NICE DAY

A young girl tingles. The tips of her fingers move gently down her face and feel soft shocks as skin barely brushes skin. Her forehead sings. Her closed eyelids leap. Fantasies play on the screen of her quivering lids and spin through a limitless playground of colors. Her fingers flick faint hairs like morning moss and the shocks sharpen. Then, like lightning, one finger lightly clips her nerve-lined lips and she tingles all over. Her whole body sings. Her soul soars. She is alive. And she calls you out into the stillness of the dew to touch her face, to behold her birth, to hear her first song. Yes, the face of the earth is fresh this morning and the fingers of God keep tickling songs, tapping life shocks, or rapping finger rhythms of red. His word-pulses vibrate through a million moist tree-tops. The birds sing where he's around. Tree-tops glisten with breath. Tree houses blossom with dreams and stories where time is a toy. The young earth summons you. Yet you may never hear her singing until you can play with time, bounce the clock down the stairs and imagine the full circle of one moment. In one moment, the lifetime of your birth, all worlds are new. We are born to imagine. Of all our six senses, imagination is the one we can least afford to lose. It keeps the other five dancing. It's every-where, like God. It's the laughter of God who surrounds us. His fingers tickle our imaginations, our senses, our souls. He is our song. So move out into the sunshine. Take off! Listen to the songs of the young girl. Taste her tingle. Say, Hi, to the newborn world. Say, Hi, to God. And have a nice day.

BE!

Some morning when the sun is lazy and the clouds have washed the earth, walk among the sparkling grass and be.

Just be!

Don't have anything else to do but be! Be what you are but be ready to be something more. Get your feet wet with wonder and be. Be open to being.

Sit at an intersection and watch the human beings. Most of them are cell people—cells not beings. A little rain speeds up the movement of the cells on the streets. They scurry from one cell to the next worrying, worrying, worrying about being "something." They are oiled by worry, slippery cells moving from room to room, car to **car park, desk** to desk, office to office, cell to cell. Behind each one there is someone else hurrying harder and blasting his horn, honking his heart. Up front there is someone hurrying a little slower for the sake of her spastic beehive hair set. Pity about the rain.

"Persons" is the magic word. They all want to be treated like persons. So we hear that "at this bank you will get the personal treatment of a 'person' not a punch card. Our punch cards will have your personal number on it saying very definitely that this number is a PERSON." And in the super cells of the computer your number may also have a personal notation like V.I.P. or sometime later R.I.P.

Before then, some morning when the sun is itching and the clouds have washed an empty tomb, walk among the sparkling grass and be.

Just be!

IF YOU LEAN BACK
(as Matthew did)

If you lean back and listen
you may hear someone breathing at your side,
almost in time with your own,
almost your shadow,
and you wonder. . . .

You wonder why that breath
seems more than breathing,
more than air rhythms,
and almost part of you. . . .

For if you lean back and listen
you can hear yourself breathing
almost in time with someone at your side,
almost touching their soul
and you wonder. . . .

You wonder whether breathing
isn't deeper than the sounds
that simmer through lips. . . .
You wonder whether maybe
every timid breath
isn't one more sweep
of someone else's spirit
moving in from somewhere else
and plunging to the depths of your body
to give you life.

Their life
and their breath
are now yours
. . . and His!

FINGER FACES
(Bob's dream)

When I was small
I could breathe
upon a cold pane
and watch the frightened faces
I had made with my fingers
slowly fade
and fly
into silk flakes of air.

Now I am tall
my snow-screened window
winks back,
like instant replay,
any face I call up
that once was mirrored
in its past.

Soon perhaps
I'll see your eyes
laughing into mine,
your face
bursting over my shoulder,
your spirit
splashing on my cheeks
and turn my window into flames
of leaping faces
that no moist glass could ever know.

When will you come
and touch my tomorrow
with your madness?
my window
with your eyes?
my face
with your fingers?

MY NAME IS "LONELY"

May I call you,
just call you
to say
"I am here"?
not to ask a favour,
tell you my troubles,
or listen to lies
but call you,
just call
like a bird in the twilight
blessing the day.

DO YOU LOVE ME?

If you should chance to ask,
"Do you love me?"
with a whisper in your eyes
much the way you did
when we were waiting young,
then I would say, "I do."
But if you ask, as once in pain,
"How do you love me now?"
what shall I say?

I'll say I cannot speak sometimes
at the door when we part
and my throat jams my tongue . . .
full of fear.
I'll mention the tearlines
that break the dust on my cheek
when once we meet again
with our lips.
I'll paint you a fantasy
born in my bones
of a girl with a tiny toy bottle
tapping the last wink of perfume
on the nape of her neck
or the edge of her bright yellow dress.
I'll paint it and love it
and wish like a child
that soft with the dusk
we would wait for the night
and not be obliged to go out,
to go out. . . .

My love may not be perfect,
but this I know,
that the face on my fingertips,
the cheeks in my hand,
and the breath in my palm
that I feel in my flesh
can only be yours
like a windsong of truth
that runs through my hair.

These lines say, "I love you."
What shall I say more,
except perhaps to tell you,
I love you even when you snore?

JOE'S WINE

(available downtown Chicago)

It's good to walk among the wise
and hear the words they leave behind
like tips on the counter.

The other day
I saw two poor old men eating bread
in the oldest parts of town.
The one man said,
"Hey, Joe,
Do you think we'll ever
amount to anything?"

At first I thought, how sad!
But then he laughed
a little
and I knew that he was laughing
at himself
and all the world that totters
on the pinnacle of sweet success.

Amount to anything?
He had!
And his wisdom
was wine for my bread.

He was someone.

SOFT DROPS

(from Barbara)

Soft drops tear through your lashes
and tumble to tremble
moist over my scorched lips
brushing your temple.

Your open soul quivers alive
at the nerve point of my tongue
and all I may breathe
deep in there
where only God's fingers run
is "Gently, dear,
gently,
I'm here."

THE SANDBOX IS SILENT

The sandbox is silent,
the playground is empty
where you played with me
as a child.

Where did you go?

I used to thank you
for birthdays and babies,
for all fluffy things
like kittens and dogs,
for all slippery things
like soap in the bath,
and for all wriggly,
muddy, bubbly things
in the garden.

Life was a wide surprise,
a hundred tomorrows
to trust
and love
as big as my birthday.

And you were right there
as close as the colours,
the sunshine,
the air.

Where did you go, God,
when I put away
my childish things,
my building bricks,
my Jesus songs,
my past?

The sandbox is silent now
and living is slow
without you.

I MISS YOU

"I miss you," he said.

There was a long pause
deep in the phone
until through the hollow
of the night
I echoed:
"I miss you, too."

That says it,
doesn't it?

As we grow,
we grow apart
from the God we knew as kids
and with a fleeting pang
we cry:
"I miss you, Lord."

Then we pull ourselves
together
and dial another number.

THE SONG OF BARBY GIST

Competition
should be like hopscotch
whoever wins
invites you
home for ice cream
in the tree house.

IN BARBY'S TREE HOUSE

Just for tonight
when the wind is quiet and lonely,
would you like to come with me
up to the tree house,
your tree house and mine,
to crawl up the ladder
and curl up on the floor
where little leaves whisper secrets
to the sky?

In a tree house
the floor is the altar,
high up like an eagle.
Here everyone sits on the altar,
high like an eagle,
like an echo.

No one wears shoes . . .
we take them off to listen
and feel the lips of the air,
the soft flutter of pine needles
that play like piccolos
when old people aren't watching.

The best thing about a tree house
is that you can pretend
and people won't laugh at you . . .
or if they do, you don't have to listen.
They won't say you're phony
or fake
or foolish.
Up here you can play, pretend,
and be yourself . . . just be yourself.

Up here you can hear
the music that stirs dreams,
bubbles like the resurrection . . .
love music, ice-cream music,
music you don't hear
except in your tree-house church
wherever it happens to be.

The sounds shake the tree
and you want to dance . . .
no, it isn't dangerous to dance
on the floor . . . on the altar . . .
it's good.
The cobwebs laugh
and the celebration hidden in your soul
bursts through your face
and your body explodes
with rhythm.

Then you sit quiet, waiting quiet,
there
and you look at each other across the floor
and see each other truly
perhaps for the first time.
You see the eyes of a friend
and you trust him . . . trust her . . .
trust enough to tell stories,
to say HI to any tree-house people you know,
little people whose lives and loves
are bigger than their size.
You can say HI, and mean it,
to Humpty Dumpty, Mary with her lamb,
and maybe even Georgie Porgie.

You can doodle on the walls
with tears and titters
and wisps of moonlight lace.

You can say what you feel,
tell tree-house poems and stories . . .
your very own!
You can sit with God
who sits beside Alice in Wonderland.
God is really quite sunny.
He has ice cream on his beard,
blackberry juice on his trousers,
and perhaps some egg on his face.
He's easier to talk to
if you promise to be yourself.

He invites you to the tree house
at the tree
where men are free.

WINDLEAF

Take off
windleaf
and dare the lightning's laugh
to halt your eagle flight from me

Take off
windleaf
and dodge the long night shadows
that haunt our muddled memories

Take off
windleaf
and fall across the rent mind
of a lonely girl in fallen leaves

Tell her
windleaf
that my tears have turned to wine
ready to be tasted under oaks

Tell her
windleaf
that I love her in her winter pain
before the snow muses its white away

IN GOD'S TREE HOUSE
(which is much like Barby's)

When God was a boy
his long black hair shone
like silence in the night.
No car fumes or beer cans
cluttered his vast tree house.
He swept like warm wings
across the eyes of the morning
calling barefoot kids
to watch him make the world.

God held his first creation that day
and kids danced in for miles
to see the newborn sky
and the bright blue rivers.

Many came and played with the sun
but no one stayed for long.
"We're getting too old and sensible
for that sort of thing," they said.

And today?
God is getting older too, they say,
and nobody of note
attends his creations anymore.
The old boy doesn't draw a crowd
the way he did at Sinai.

It's regrettable indeed, they add,
that the delicate work of his hands
is obscured by the smog,
that obscene neon signs
hide his heavens,
that muttering landmines
drown the mating call of the cricket,
or that sewerage-slick seas
discolour the ocean flowers.

But, well, God is getting older,
and we can't expect his miracles
to be as brilliant as before.
God looks older too, they say.
His face is pocked with atomic scars
and his hair is a ghostly gray.
But that's to be expected.
After all, he must have aged a thousand years
when they killed his boy
at the battle of Calvary.

They're cutting down his tree houses now
to make way for parking lots
and twenty-story tombs
called high-rise heavens.

But should you escape
this enormous cement cemetery
and hear the sun fling love
across your howling thoughts,
or find a recent raindrop
balanced on a petal,
you might see the young face of God
reflected like silence in the sun.

And you may hear again
his call to dance in his tree house
where slender white banners
fly forth in the wind
like streamers of black light,
like dreams of sunshine,
like ribbons for a new world
ready to be unwrapped.

And if you go there
don't be surprised
if the banners look like the shrouds
that once graced the torn body
of God's risen boy.

For in that tree house
where God holds his creations
all men are young
and faith goes barefoot.

MERRY
CRABGRASS

That
crazy
crabgrass
Lord
it
keeps
crawling
up
through
old
cracks
we
so
carefully
sealed
with
cement
and
it
giggles
there
in
the
gravel
as
if
it
knows
something
about
. . .
the
future

MERRY
CRABGRASS

2

Hi!
Have a
Good Friday

IN THE NAME OF THE FATHER

Leader: Father of the lonely man,

People: We are lonely, so lonely.

Leader: Father of that lonely Son,

People: We are lonely, lonely sons.

Leader: Father, our Father,

People: We are with your Son today.

Leader: Lonely, lonely Father,

People: We are here in pain.
We are waiting in pain.
And we remember your pain.

Leader: Lonely Father, lonely Son.

People: Reach us. Touch us.
Be with us. Love us.
That's all we ask today.

Leader: Lonely Father, lonely Son,
lonely Spirit of the night,
lonely, lonely, Three-in-One.

People: In the mystery of your loneliness
help us through the night.

Leader: Father of the lonely,

People: Let us never die in lonely pain
as Jesus died today
and other sons have died
again and again and again.

Leader: Amen.

People: Amen.

HAVE A GOOD FRIDAY

A young girl flinches and I feel the pain. A flinch, a tear, a twitch, and the needle is in. For an instant I know her. And she knows the bite of her heritage. Her feet and hands are bleeding. She has walked in the wake of her parents' wealth where death and deceit, war and waste are scattered like broken glass. A young girl flinches and a young man dies. The young learn only too soon about age. The poor bypass puberty. The wealthy don't want it. And the average kid has little chance for carefree fantasy. His youth dies young. He grabs for life with all the gusto he can get. He clutches at the ornaments. There is no New Year . . . only NOW! He goes round only once in life . . . never twice. He tastes the tongues of racist friends. He fears the loneliness of insecure leaders. He flinches and he vomits. He watches squares playing blocks with land and lives. And he smells death in the playpen. He sees death on his street, his screen, his horizon . . . and the crucifixion makes sense. The young, the young like you, still come to Calvary by one road or another. But they come to see a young man die. Their Christ is not an old bachelor of thirty-three. He's a youth. He went round three times in life. In three short years he lived three lifetimes of love, revolution, and death. He died at the hands of the system called man.

You come to Calvary when you feel the marks of dying fresh in your own flesh. You come if the suffering King is more than a sentimental ache. You identify with a broken friend when you touch him with your own agonies. When you touch you listen in. The seven words from the cross become thundering torments. And you flinch. I know, for I have watched with you. And a few of your feelings are reflected here. They are offered for our good in Lent, on the Friday called good, or any day of human passion. Use them for a three-hour service or three years of listening. The Lord flinches, turns, and whispers, "Have a good Friday." T.G.I.F.*

* (Thank God it's Friday).

BEHOLD THE MAN

(. . . wherever he is dying)

Gentle Jesus meek and mild.
Well, that's the way we learned it.
That's the way it sounded in Sunday school.
Jesus was like a huge heavenly teddy bear
waiting to welcome us to our playhouse in heaven.

Church didn't change that much.
We sang, "Jesus the very thought of thee
                With sweetness fills the breast. . . . "

How sweet it was!
But we grow up a little and something turns sour.
Even the name "Jesus" is not as comfortable to say
as a more general word like God or Lord.

Well, what about J.C.?
Is he really a tender touch for kids
or a rough revolutionary for God?
Why should he let some neurotic woman
wipe his sweaty feet with her hair?

Anyway, we don't really expect him to return,
at least not for a long time.
After all, it's been two thousand years since he left
and anyone who came storming in on the clouds
the way he predicted about himself
would probably be taken for a lost astronaut.

But what if he were around?
Where would we see him?

Would he be a disc jockey or a plumber?
Would he be a cowboy or an Indian?
Would he march on Washington
or would Washington march on him?

Then again, perhaps he never really left us.
Or perhaps he checked in secretly
and no one actually saw him return.
Perhaps he's on death row,
skid row,
or the back row of your church?

I wonder, if we were to look closely enough,
listen intently enough,
and walk far enough from our cozy corners
we might find him suffering for us . . .
waiting for us to say, "That's him!"
"That's J.C."

BEHOLD YOUR SON
(a litany for those
who dare to look)

Leader: There he hangs,
King of the criminals,
Lord of the laughing mob,
Master of the militants,
Protector of the prostitutes,
Friend of the freaks,
Hero of the heroin addicts.
Do you want him?

People: Yes, we want him.
He is our man.
He lived in our corners,
our holes, our ghettos.
And he died for our camp
to take from our camp
any who want to go with him.

Leader: There he dies,
a traitor, a fool
and a country clown
on his wild way to God
inviting all to come along:
"Today you can have it all.
Today you can have it all."
Do you want him?

People: Yes, we want him.
For we confess today
that we are not ashamed
to identify that man
as the very Son of God
who gives the injured life,
and the very Man of men
who makes each man his brother.

Mother,
look at your little boy now,
look at his clumsy clothes,
his hysterical hair,
and the dull dream in his eyes.

Is that your son?
Will you be his mother now?

BEHOLD YOUR SON
(. . . or for Mother's Day)

You, Mother,
why does he hate your world,
your chrome-plated kitchen,
your bright plastic flowers,
your armchair decisions
to invest in a firm
that will suck poor men dry
and help young men die
of napalm burns
or bullets in the brain?

Yes, Mother,
were you polishing the brass
when he wanted your love?

Or is it your world,
this technological trap,
this system, this machine
that grinds you to be
a go-go girl
with nowhere to go?

Look at your little boy now,
burning his draft card
or wishing he had the guts to burn it,
looking for someone who is honest enough
to admit the smut in his soul
and the long phony prayer
to old Santa Claus
who jokes through his beard,
"That's my boy!"

Mother,
Behold your son!

I THIRST

Will you walk with me in there? Will you come with me into the angry wounds of the city? Or will you run scared? Before you run, kid, smell the anger rising. Hear the broken glass singing sharp and dry.

The anger swells like stale yeast caught tight in the chest. The pavement heat scratches the skin and waits for blood to burn. On every person you pass you can smell it—stale human anger, swelling, brooding.

You can smell it as you feel your own gut pull into its pit. And you feel like screaming JESUS CHRIST because a little kid just did. He yelled it and meant it. His brothers are spraying black paint on the walls and saying, FREE BOBBY or KILL WHITEY or NIGGER LOVER. And all the shadows seem to have strange orange faces.

Life is under siege for that kid and every kid here. The cruising cops, boarded storefronts, grilled windows, and coughing trucks are only sorry tokens of lost promises. This is the pit. God holds his breath here and only the broken glass sings sharp in the light.

I guess God is waiting for someone like Jesus Christ to come and cut his feet here. Anyone who hopes to save the city will need to be ready to die from broken glass.

But you, if you walk down any street of your town on a hot day, you may smell the anger. Once it becomes stale the glass will sing. And you'll get very thirsty.

Lord, how in this hell do we find the courage to enter the pits of life and be salt for glass wounds? How can we be Christ to angry men when we are chicken with our brothers?

Lord, I thirst.

TODAY YOU WILL BE WITH ME IN. . . .
(after the Pakistan typhoon disaster)

God,
you killed hundreds of thousands
of worshiping men and women
in one vicious night
in Pakistan.

For a while you wanted them,
warmed them with breath,
burnished them with sunshine,
and prepared them
to die.

A tender tornado,
a gentle earthquake,
a breath of lightning
seem like reasonable reminders
of your muscle power
on earth.

But what kind of kicks
do you get from a cyclone
of swirling filth
and mud
and death
churning in a wild swill?

Well?

Is that your sadistic way
of thinning out the population
as it swells and swells
in tight corners of earth?
Do you like the smell of dying,
the feel of lime
on bloated corpses?
Do you relish rotting rice,
the frozen eyes of starving babies
staring you down?

But why Pakistan?
Why not New York
or Texas
or London
or me?
Do you have to keep stirring Job's whirlwind

to prove you are God?
Do you need to kill thousands
to remind us
of how you killed your own son
for us . . . and for them?

Or is it You, God,
who needs reminding
about your boy?

Sorry, Lord,
I guess I didn't mean that.
I'll try to understand your words
for the dying . . .
warm words of hope:

"Today,
you will be with me in Pakistan."

Today,
cyclone day,
whirlwind day,
world-disaster day,
you will be with me in . . . Paradise.

Let me never forget
the bloated faces
of my brothers in the vicious mud,
the burning flesh
or the angry face of my Lord . . .
or are they the same today?

Today. . . .

For nine months
we enjoyed the company
of

(MARK ANDERSON)

On February 3, he was

born dead

born dead

born dead

born dead

born dead

Lord, men are born to die
    in slum ratholes
    in highway crashes
    in Vietnam ambushes
    in campus riots.

Lord, is it better to be
    born dead?

Lord, when I say "born dead"
    it's like saying
    Hallelujah and Damn
    in the same breath.

Lord, help me to say "born dead"
    and slowly add the words,
    "Today, thou shalt be with
    me . . . in . . . par . . . ."

Lord, I can't say them.
    How could you?

TODAY THOU SHALT BE WITH ME IN PARADISE

FATHER, FORGIVE THEM

I often lose yesterday's laughter
in the dusk
until there is barely the faintest feeling
of value
in all the hours I've lived
and loved
and lost.

Somewhere I blew it.
I wronged my home,
my family,
my friends,
myself.

"I forgive you all your wrongs."
"Just be yourself and pray."
"All you need is love."
"I forgive you every day."

I hear those voices
but it's hard to believe
they are you, Lord.
You may forgive
But I can't forget.
My insides won't let me forget
. . . to say nothing of my friends.

Who trusts a thief,
a stranger,
a liar,
a loser like me
at the Lord's table
kneeling very close.

Who accepts the kiss of peace
from a kid like me
who keeps thinking about sex.

Who forgives a fool?
Who forgets? Who?

It's only the laughter
of yesterday's love
that fades.
The wrongs rarely die,
even on the cross, Lord,
even on the cross.

Help me forget . . . and forgive.

Father, forgive them
for they should have known better.

FATHER, FORGIVE US

(a litany for listening)

Leader: Dear Father, voices of agony surround me.

People: We've heard them for years.

Leader: I hear the voice of the earth
defiled and torn by our own greedy hands.

People: We don't want to listen.

Leader: I hear the voice of struggling peoples,
seething with anger against their oppressors.

People: We don't want to listen.

Leader: I hear the voice of silent martyrs,
black mothers and homeless fathers,
beaten children and forgotten elders.

People: We don't want to listen.

Leader: I hear the voice of men on earth
poisoned by their own fears,
caught in their own selfishness,
dying in their own passions.

People: We're too tired to listen.

Leader: I hear a vast crowd chanting,
"We don't want to listen.
We don't want to listen."

People: Forgive us and get it over with.

Leader: I hear the voice of a dying man,
a still small voice whispering,
"Father, are these the people
I'm supposed to forgive?"

People: What did you say?

Leader: Father, forgive us
for refusing to listen.

IT IS FINISHED
(to Martin Luther King)

I walked,
an angry angel I,
across the burnt face of Eden
veiled in morbid smog
nudging the ground with tears
until I saw
an open grave before my feet,

a hollow socket in the sod,
a cold deep black mirror
whispering empty
        empty
        empty unto death.

Then I knew,
a human angel I,
the king of the garden was dead,
the trees were burnt by bullets
and one man was crucified again
without the honour of wood
        of crown
        of sacred thorns.

I needed,
ambitious angel I,
a pair of shoulders for my hands,
flesh and blood to grasp,
a solid person in the night,
the touch of human breathing
on my lips
        eyes
        tears of terror.

Silently
I heard the black explode
and mirror fragments fly
before a shouting voice
that cleft the deep,
"I have a dream," cried God,
"that man is worth the loving,
that man lives on
beyond this smoking garden
where hasty angels
swing their flaming swords
in the name of human justice!"

But the only echo ringing
through my torn heart
when all the smoke had cleared
was, "It is finished
        finished
        finished!"

LORD, I NEED A BLOOD BROTHER

(or why hast thou forsaken me?)

Lord,
I need a blood brother or sister,
the kind of true companion
that I can trust with my life
full of broken promises
and deep falls.

I don't need a friend
who will bleed for me
as much as I need someone strong,
who won't get ill when I bleed
or laugh at the foolish wrongs
who gnaw at me like demons.

Some of those I trusted
with my sins and suffering
spilled them out like water
in the wind.

Is there any human soul
who can drink the cup of my mistakes
and not toast them one night
when drunk
or lonelier than I . . .
trying to get even?

Could I trust myself
not to betray my friends
when I was broken by them?
Have I abandoned others
and left myself to be
alone with me?

NO!
There must be someone beyond this sham,
someone who will take off to find me
when I break the silence.

Is there someone listening
as my cup overflows
with unspoken private pity,
unsaid failures,
unkind thoughts?

Is there someone listening
who trusted men,
died with you, Lord,
and rose again?

Is there someone forsaken
who will not forsake me?

Or is the evil even worse?
Is mine the kind of weak pride
that will not let its weakness fall
like limp limbs
at the feet of a friend?

Lord, have I even the courage,
the red blood of human feelings,
to speak myself forth
and be a blood brother
or sister?

Are you listening, Lord?
Are you bleeding?
I am!
And I need someone to listen.

Or have you forsaken me too?

Courtesy of the Kodak International Newspaper Snapshot Awards

FORSAKEN

Leader: God. Forsaker. Father.

People: There is no more vicious word
in all the world
than the word "forsaken."

Leader: There is no more cruel scene
in all the world
than the Lord forsaken.

People: There is no more pathetic figure
in all the world
than this man forsaken.

Leader: Forsaken by the beautiful.

People: Forsaken by the merciful.

Leader: Forsaken by his friends.

People: Forsaken by his God.

Leader: Forsaken by the children.

People: Forsaken by the forsaken.

Leader: Why did you forsake him God?
Why did you forsake your Son?

People: Let him be forsaken for us.
Let him be rejected for us.

Leader: God. Forsaker. Father.

People: Never let us be forsaken again.

Leader: Father. Father. Father.

People: Amen, Father, amen.

INTO THY HANDS
(or traces of the wind)

The Zuni Indians tell
of how man and woman were made
when two tassled ears of corn,
one white, one yellow,
were placed between two buckskins.
The ancient wind of life
blew softly through those skins
until the ears were formed
as man and woman in love.
And should you look this hour
at your own fingertips
you will see traces of the wind
that first gave life to man.

Let us call across the years
to the day of our creation
out of clay,
out of corn,
out of love.
Let us ask the gentle wind
to trace the lines of life
in our silent fingertips,
in a sudden mushroom ring,
in glittering ribbon falls,
in murmuring fields of corn.

Let us feel the breath of life
warm upon our eyes and see,
as our Indian fathers saw,
the traces of our God
rising from the soul of all
to shimmer on the surface
like the dew.

Or is it too late?
Can the white man of the West
ever feel the spirit
in the touch of his dirty hands?

Are there still songs of hope
where the pride of a man
has been burnt
with the corn and the woods
that are part of his soul?

Can our Indian fathers show us
more than the traces of war,
oil-slick streams,
and fume-filled highways?
Can they teach us of God
before they die a lingering death
on the cross of our civilization?

Father, into thy hands
I commend my spirit
to feel the traces of the wind.

FROM THY HANDS

Leader: What have we done with your creation, Lord?

People: What have we done with your world?

Leader: We have filled your firmament with fumes
and your sky with poisonous gases.

People: We have lifted mushroom clouds to the heavens
and towers of Babel to belch forth "incense."

Leader: We spew our sewerage into the sea
and pervert your rivers with greasy garbage.

People: We baptize the land with cruel chemicals
and mangle the face of the earth.

Leader: Cries of anger now ring from heaven

People: And we are afraid.

Leader: Dying creatures moan in the ocean

People: And we feel sick.

Leader: For we are guilty of corrupting the sky

People: And cursing the ground with plagues.

Leader: Open your hands to heal our crimes.

People: Open your hands to heal our lives.

Leader: Send your Spirit through the soil.

People: To create our world anew.

Leader: Send your Spirit through our bodies

People: And let its traces never fade.

Leader: For from your hands we come

People: And into your hands we commend our spirits.

RESURRECTION CITY
(Washington, D.C., 1968, and . . .)

Resurrections
are no
big deals.

We hurt
and suffer hell
and hate ourselves
until we die deep inside

Still deeper somewhere
resurrection
catches us
unawares

We rise
almost unnoticed
like a quiet dawn
like the silence
after a sigh
like a child
with a toy watch
warm on a worn shoulder

Walk to the window
and wonder
at the tints
of a risen Lord
unnoticed
raising up friends
and hidden hopes
in the daze of death
on bloody sidewalks

Real resurrections
say no
to big deals

3

Hi!
Have a
Purple Lemon

THE PURPLE LEMON GAME

(to be played before or during a very dull service)

Once upon a time
when the birds ate lime
and the world was full of questions,
a purple lemon fell
from heaven or from hell
in the lap of the United Nations.

Said the lemon so purple
with a deep purple burple,
"I am giving this world three wishes.
For the magic of my juice
can reveal to you the truth
if you can agree on the issues."

The United States said,
off the top of its head,
"I think we should mass-produce it."
But the Russians wouldn't go
for purple lemon snow
if it purpled the people who use it.

"Lemons cannot talk,"
was the main German squawk,
"and they don't drop down from heaven.
We must first research
its breath and its birth
to see if this lemon's a lemon."

They set up committees,
pro and con lemonittees,
who think that lemons give wishes,
when along came a boy
who thought it a toy
and couldn't care less about issues.

If I were that boy
who thought it a toy
I'd play with that lemon all day,
I'd . . . .
Or . . . .
and . . . .

In other words it's up to you to finish the story, squeeze out your own ending,
and play with the lemon. But there is magic in the mind of anyone who figures
out three great wishes to change his world, for he might start doing just that.
Yes, if I were a boy who had a purple lemon I would. . . . Then again, when
God was a boy he. . . . Now if I were God . . . .well, go ahead and squeeze!!
Have a purple lemon.

HI, MAN : AN OPENING HYMN

Lyrics by Norman Habel
Music by Richard Koehneke

1. Hi, Man! Have a nice day, And greet me with love on the way---, For Christ is a-ris-en And that's e-nough rea-son To cel-e-brate life ev'ry day----. live high on your ho-ly, live high on your ho-ly, live high on your ho-ly feast.

2.
Hi, Man! Go climb a tree
And tell all the closed hearts you see:
Like rich old Zacchaeus
The Master can free us
To break out and break bread and be!

3.
Hi, Man! Let's go to town!
Our God can be black white or brown;
Our sin is forgiven
And that's enough reason
To turn this old world upside down.

4.
Hi, Lord! Teach us to see
The clues where your presence might be,
In faces or roses
Or like poor old Moses
A voice from a very hot tree.

5.
Hi, Man! Laugh with the weeds!
Their secret is hid in their seeds.
Your daisies are waiting
To see Christ creating
A new world where bullets are beads.

6.
Hi, Lord! Come be our guest,
Your table has only the best.
Your life blood, Lord Jesus,
Has totally freed us
To live high on your holy feast.

BORN FREE: A BAPTISMAL SHOUT

I am free!

I was born free.
No, I didn't free myself.
I entered the waters of death
and I drowned.
I died with Christ,
and Christ died with me.
We went through hell together.

But His tomb is also a womb.
The waters of death
are also waters of life.
He was there.
He spoke to the waters of the deep
and life began,
when the world was first born
and I was freeborn.

I was born free.
I rose with Christ
like a spring from the deep,
like an infant from the womb,
like a new first man.

I rose a new me,
a new man,
a free king.

People keep telling me
that I'm not really free.
My old me keeps reminding me
of wrongs I do each day:
"You're fooling yourself.
You aren't really free."

Oh, but I am!
We all are.
We were born free in baptism.
We rose free in Christ.
And He is free to free all men.
We are free!
No sin, law, old self,
or new fear,
can ever bind us forever.

Never! Never! Never!
We ARE born free.
WE ARE!

OUR THUNKS TO TWO DRUNKS

I saw two drunks come sailing in
on Christmas Day in the morning,
sailing into Forty-second Street,
across the oily ice
rolling them like eyeballs loose,
two splattered sprawls,
run aground,
victims of their drunken squalls . . . two friendly drunks
                                         two flattened failures
                                         two brave men!

One failure spoke with slow
and loving voice:
    Olfriend
        nowletme
            helpyou
                UP!
His failing friend,
well drowned in self-pity,
spluttered similar kind thoughts:
    Comeonnow
        lean
            onme!
    Hangon!
        Hangon!
            ForChrisake, HANG ON!

Two leaning hanging men,
almost erect by the grace of each other,
sailing forth on Forty-second Street
like a strange four-legged ship,
singing lustily
tossing to and fro
        fro and to
        down and up
                up against the slippery sea,
                up to celebrate the season,
                up to celebrate the spirit

                        of another brave man,
                        an even greater failure
                        flattened to a mast
                        and hanging on a crossbar
                        with me.

FOR PEOPLE IN PIECES

A CONFESSION

Leader: In the name of the Father who makes us,
in the name of the Son who makes us free,
in the name of the Spirit who makes us one,

Response: Amen.

Leader: In the beginning God had a plan for this world
where He was King and everything was together,

Response: Sunshine and tigers, daisies and children,
everything was together as it should be.

Leader: But the world did not stay together;
things were torn apart like the pieces of a puzzle,

Response: And they are still being torn apart today.

Leader: Our world is being torn apart by war and pollution,

Response: People are torn apart by fear and hate,

Leader: Children are torn apart from their parents;

Response: And each of us is torn apart inside.

Leader: We are like torn pieces of God's vast puzzle

Response: And we need help.

AND ABSOLUTION:

Leader: But our Lord Jesus Christ came into this our world
to put this puzzle together.
That's why he says to us today:
"I love you."

Response: "I love you as you are."

Leader: "I am healing you."

Response: "I am healing your torn lives and torn world."

Leader: "I am putting you back together."

Response: "I am putting everything back together."

Leader: "You are all precious parts of God's puzzle.
You are His sons and daughters."

Response: "So celebrate! Be children and celebrate!"

Leader: Amen!

Response: Amen! Amen! Amen!

HI, HAVE A PURPLE LEMON : AN INTROIT

The Lemon Squeezer *(or Leader)*   **The Purple Juicers** *(or Response)*

Hi!
Have a purple lemon!
Have a purple lemon
Fly your carpet mind
And ask if God is free
To make a magic world
Where blue people laugh

Hi!
A pure purple lemon!
Or a bright red banana!
To the talking tree of God
To come and play "create,"
Where purple lemons swim,
And have a nice day.

Yes, have a nice day
For the night is forgiven
The soul of the earth
Are waiting for us

And bounce it like a ball,
And the morning is free,
And the breath of the sun
To have a nice day.

Shall we dance with the wind
Shall we dance with the rain
Shall we dance with the snow
Shall we dance with each other

As it ripples the clouds?
As it tickles the grass?
As it muffles the night?
And have a nice day?

Let's talk to the trees
Toast an old turtle
Spin tales with spiders
Then laugh with a jackass

And celebrate sparrows!
And praise porcupines!
And salute an old goat!
And have a purple day.

Why not hail a long nose
Kiss a double chin
The Maker doesn't stare
So let's call him in to play

Or bless a bald head?
Or rock with knees that knock?
At the way He made us all.
And have a nice day.

Let's splash through a puddle
Or grow a few grapes
Work in fields of rice
Risk a little love
Add a little singing

And walk on the water,
And turn water into wine,
And feed five thousand
And have a purple lemon
For purple lemonade.

All purple praise to God
All purple to the Spirit

And all purple to His Son
Every purple lemon day.

PSALM 23 : AN OLD TESTAMENT READING
(as said by the Establishment)

We are your shepherds, you'll never ever want.
We make you to lie down in cement pastures,
We lead you by polluted waters,
We psychoanalyze your soul.
We lead you in the ways of warfare
        for our country's sake.
Yea, though you walk through the shadow of the ghetto
        of city hall,
You need fear no muggings,
Our billy clubs and our binoculars will protect you.
We prepare a million-dollar plate dinner
In the presence of the starving,
We anoint your head with degrees
Your report card overflows with A's.
Surely law and order will follow you
        all the days of your life
And you will dwell in the establishment forever.

OLD ADAM—NEW EVE: AN EPISTLE

(Kathy's cry for freedom)

"Sugar and spice
and everything nice,
that's what little girls are made of."

We've been told that so often
we almost believe it.

When I was a kid I wanted building bricks
not dainty dolls or nurse kits.
I wanted to be a doctor
but they suggested I clean bedpans.
I wanted to study history and maths
but they suggested art and typing.
I wanted to play football
but they suggested playing house.

So I sat home with my acne
watching the Miss World Pageant.
I was surrounded by "everything nice":
"Sex and the Single Girl,"
"The Joys of Motherhood,"
Playboy centrefolds,
T.V. soap wives,
Racquel Welch, Julie Christie,
and hundreds of pretty faces
that weren't anything like me.

Why should I be a woman
if I have to giggle to be noticed,
wiggle to be wanted
and made-up to the eyelashes
to make my way up the ladder
for a job that will pay
half what any man would get?

Why can't I be a woman
who is really a woman,
a woman who is me,
a woman who is a person
and not a "nice girl,"
a woman who is free
to speak and live and laugh
like any man.

Why can't I be treated as a person
whose worth is myself not my sex,
whose power is me as me.

Lord, wasn't I created free
instead of nice,
me instead of mud?

Liberate me, Lord.
Free me from the old Adam
and create a new Eve within me.

A GRADUAL FOR KIDS

I watched a little girl
in the lazy rain
kick an empty beer can
home from school.

Fool!
. . .with new shoes
no less.
. . .with new shoes
no more!

Those shoes were never
cast in bronze.
No sir!

But there's a glorious pile
of leather-beaten beer cans
waiting
behind her house
just for kicks.

MATTHEW 2:1—12: A GOSPEL FOR LAUNCHINGS

U.F.O.'s are dangerous.
If you follow them
they can lead you almost anywhere.

I've always said you need proof.
For anything way-out like that
you need proof.

Like those three vagabond scientists
from the East
who had a thing
about a star-style U.F.O.
and followed
a less-than-scientific theory
that their little light
was a superindication
of some other strange development.

Psychedelic dreamers!

They checked with official sources
in Jerusalem
who hastily checked the records
for any information
on the location
of possible uprisings.

The scientists were advised to report back
in appropriate form,
in triplicate form,
whereupon an unofficial gang of officials
would be dispatched with political blessings
to investigate the scene
and cloud the issue.

The scientists
reached a place called Bethlehem
and disappeared mysteriously
leaving their wallets,
their identification cards,
their credit cards,
their astrology notebooks,
their visas,
and almost everything.

Rumor has it they found an infant,
identified him,
worshipped him,
took off,
and forgot about the U.F.O.

U.F.O.'s are certainly dangerous.

A
PURPLE
IF

If
I
were
the
finger
of
God
and
all
the
world
were
ticklish. . . .

A LITANY FOR LEARNING WHEN TO LAUGH

Lord, teach us to laugh as you laughed long ago
     When the sound of your laughter made heaven and earth,
When you juggled the spheres that now bounce across space
     and played with the clay that you formed into man,
When you painted the colours with sunshine and rain
     And rode roaring dragons like storms in the sea;
Lord, teach us to laugh with the world you enjoy,
     To laugh with the sun as it softens the soil,
With whirlwinds and windmills that tickle the sky,
     With bright yellow daisies that wink at the clouds,
With penguins who smile at the way humans walk,
     With mockingbirds mocking the way that we talk,
With laughing hyenas who leap sleeping lions,
     With monkeys who slide down the necks of giraffes;
Lord, teach us to laugh from the depths of our selves,
     And give us the faith of one mustard seed,
Tell us the secret of the great Pumpkin Seed
     Who laughs every night in his orange balloon,
Teach us to laugh at our silly mistakes,
     The length of our nose or the shape of our face,
To laugh at ourselves instead of our friends,
     To laugh like a child with a wild whirling kite;
Lord, teach us to hear as the stone rolls away,
     The sound of your laughter ring out through the night,
And teach us to feel when our spirits are low
     That you laughed in the face of old death for us all;
Lord, teach us to laugh and teach us to be
     Alive in your life, for your laughter is free!

A HYMN FOR LAUGHING AT LEVIATHAN*

*(or any other oppressive power—to the
melody of Battle Hymn of the Republic)*

God's love moved across the waters of the deep,
God's love laughed and ev'ry life began to leap,
God's love last laughed at monsters meant to creep
Like old Leviathan,
                    and we are. . .

            Free to feel the Spirit's laughter,
            Free to find our inner laughter,
            Free to hear the risen laughter
            of HIM who's really free!

Move through, move aside, today is women's day,
Move through, laugh aloud with weak and poor and gay,
Laugh, laugh, laugh at ev'ry monstrous power play
Of old Leviathan,
                    and we are. . .

Christ's love moves amid the fog of fear and doubt,
Christ's death frees up even prisoners to shout,
Christ's laugh flushes ev'ry ugly power out
Like old Leviathan,
                    and we are. . .

Look up, Leviathan, the birds are moving in,
Flip out, Leviathan, your power cannot win,
Turn round, Leviathan, and take it on the chin
With resurrection joy,
                    and we are. . .

*Leviathan was a violent violet dragon of old who represented the ugly waters
of chaos that threatened to destroy the earth. In some Old Testament texts he
is the symbol of oppressive powers like Egypt. The God of Israel clobbered
that monster and rendered him as harmless as "Puff, the Magic Dragon." He is
God's toy, His rubber duck in Ps. 104:25—26. Leviathan is like an enormous
purple lemon that God rides through the ocean while He laughs. Every time
Leviathan comes to life as a repressive power in your community remember
his past fate, sing this song and laugh. He's deflatible!

(One day take a good look into
your garbage cans and offer this)

TO THE GODS OF OUR GARBAGE CANS:
A GENERAL PRAYER

Kids: Good gods,

Adults: Good and gracious gods of the garbage can

Kids: Lift your lids

Adults: And hear our prayer.

Kids: We have given you our best

Adults: In sacred plastic sacks.

Kids: Gods of our garbage cans,

Adults: Have mercy on us.

Kids: Gods of our garbage cans,

Adults: Be open to our cry.

Kids: Continental Insurance Co.,

Adults: Save us from sin.

Kids: Continental Can Co.,

Adults: Preserve us with tin.

Kids: Time magazine,

Adults: Give us more time.

Kids: Playboy magazine,

Adults: Give us more ads
to give us more things
that give us more time
to have more life.

Kids: Dear Life,

Adults: Send us 25 weeks of life
for $2.95.

Kids: Dear Wall Street,

Adults: Are stocks in heaven up?

Kids: Dear A & P,

Adults: Are steaks in hell tough?

Kids: Dear White House,

Adults: Keep our spirits up.

Kids: Diet Rite Cola,

Adults: Keep me looking slim
to the very end.

Kids: Arrid Extra Dry,

Adults: Keep my odor in
to the very end.

Kids: And when my last hour has come

Adults: As our god puts on his lid

Kids: As we move all the way up to Cool
and we prepare to meet our friends above;

Adults: Old I.B.M. and S.S.T.,
Johnny Walker and L.S.D.,

Kids: As we face our last Master Charge

Adults: Ready to watch that TV in the sky,

Kids: American Express,

Adults: Speed us on our way.

Kids: Avis, Avis,

Adults: Help us try harder.

Kids: United Airlines,

Adults: Make us fly faster.

Kids: Faster faster

Adults: Faster faster

Kids: Alka Seltzer

Adults: Faster faster

Kids: Dodge Charger

Adults: Faster faster

Kids: Boeing Boeing

Adults: Faster faster

Kids: Apollo Fifteen

Adults: Faster faster

Kids: Garbage Master

Adults: Faster faster

Kids: Fast!

Adults: For there's a very old man
on a very old horse
who keeps gaining on us.

EASTER EXPERIMENTS: A NON-SERMON

(and the way things are going we could do
with a few more non-sermons for sermons)

Some people are born under the sign of the egg
and should be classified as experiments,
fermenting Easter experiments
that must be kept carefully controlled.

What else can you call abnormal people
who throw together a bunch of odd ideas
and produce all kinds of comical reactions
in their lives.

First of all they take J.C.,
bury him in a cool cave,
seal it like a capsule,
open it three days later,
and begin to examine the evidence.

Now the evidence is
one very long bandage (perhaps black or white),
one very large rock (probably round),
one very missing body (belonging to J.C.),
one bunch of hysterical women (of questionable repute),
a series of wild stories (about angels and voices),
a number of changed people (like fishermen and fools),
and a mystery (which remains a mystery).

Now you can explain this evidence in several ways:
Someone stole the body of J.C.
And started a rumour about his return OR
J.C. was never really dead
but revived and played the game OR

there was a false bottom in the cave
and he escaped to another hideout OR
Jesus went straight to hell
and returned as a ghost to plague his murderers OR. . . .

Anyway resurrection stories
are as old as God himself.
If God were dead and rose again
it wouldn't be the first time, or the last,
. . . if we believe the record.

But you have to be careful
because God doesn't prevent these experiments
from reacting in society
and shouting HE IS RISEN.
They believe that story about J.C.
"Psst! Did you hear the latest?" they say.
"Well, Jesus rose the other day."

You ask, "Why?"
and they say "Why not?"
I'll tell you why not.

It's never really happened
and it doesn't happen now.
Everything has to die and decay.
That's life. . .or rather death!
But these ridiculous Easter experiments
keep bouncing up and down on earth shouting,
"We have risen.
We rose with him
and he rose with us.
He started it all
and the chain reaction is spreading."

"He rose," they say,
"and breathed his new spirit in people.
You can't kill that spirit
because it changes old spirits
with a hidden power from the empty cave
that swirls everywhere
in a chain reaction . . .
one! two! three! four!"

These experiments are rather unsettling
and someone had better control them. . .soon.

I'm thankful, however, that most Christians
don't really trust God enough
to keep the experiment alive;
if they did the whole world might explode
with experiments
in one enormous uncontrollable Easter.

THE COMING OF THE GREAT BUBBLE:
A CHANCE(L) DRAMA

(or a slight communication gap)

Kid: Hey can you see it? Can you? Look everybody.
There it is. Big and round and eternal and groovy.
There it is. The one we've been waiting for.
Look. . . can you see it coming down the highway. . .
Can you?

Cop: Move along kid.

Kid: Can you see it? Can you?

Cop: Just keep moving.

Kid: You bet I will, man. . .moving and swinging around that
big bubble. . . .

Cop: What did you say?

Kid: I'm following a big bubble, big boy. . . .Got it? Dig?

Cop: A bubble?

Kid: Over there. . .see. . .high. . .like man, it's the most,
it says love, joy, peace. . .it says everything. . . .

Cop: What I say is MOVE . . . .

Kid: Now look officer. . .I'm just doing my thing.

Cop: Well don't do it here. . .it messes up the street.

Kid: You just aren't with it?

Cop: I'm damned if I want to be with a bubble.

Kid: Oh, it's not just a bubble. . .it's love. . .love. . .
All you need is love. . .and you can make the scene.

Cop: Well, I'll tell you. . .you dirty little punk. . .you need a
lot more than love when it gets down to 5° below. . . .

Kid: No, no, love is like now, way out. . .out of sight. . .
Like that big beautiful bubble of happiness and understanding
and acceptance and peace. . .like it's out of sight when you
catch the vision. . .out of sight. . . .

Cop: Well, I'll buy that. I can't see anything either.

Kid: No. . .you gotta go and feel it. . .let your soul reach out like
the sound waves. . .and blow your mind. . . .

Cop: I don't know about blowing your mind, but if you don't move
I'll beat your brains in.

Kid: You don't dig. But I love you. . .I'm trying to accept you as
a person. . .like human, person-to-person. . .and you don't want
to try and understand me. . .hey, I'm trying. . .I'm a beautiful
person. . .

Cop: Yeah, sure, you look like Jesus. . .and you smell like
Lazarus:

Kid: No look, man, up there. . .it's the real. . .the ultimate. . .the one
way. . .be yourself. . .be a person. . .be free. . .and love,
love. . .that's the way. . .the solution. . .the dream. . .and we'll
have no more war.

Cop: You been drinkin'?

Kid: No. . .why?

Cop: Smoking pot?

Kid: No. . .I'm clean. Like why? I've been trying to convert you. . .
to get you to see the light, man. . .the bubble. . .the dream. . .
Accept me, man. . .don't fight it. . .love. . .not acid. . .love.

Cop: You're high. . .and you're blocking the traffic. . .I'm going to
take you in if you don't move along and stop pointing up at
that weather balloon. . .

Kid: That's no weather balloon. . .it's the love bubble. . . .All you
need is love, man. . . .

Cop: Will you move. . .and take all this gang of punks with
you or will I go and get an escort. . .???

Kid: We stay, man, we'll worship the sound, the feel, the taste
. . .we're here till the soul of tomorrow. . .we're in with
the dream. . .hang loose officer. . .hang loose.

Cop: All right. . .I'm too uptight to fight
and I ain't had enough juice to hang loose,
But when I come back with my boys
there's going to be a hell of a hole
in the soul of your bubble. Goodnight.

(Prepared with the help of kids in Williamsport, Pa.)

THE COMING OF THE DREAMBUSTERS
(or a second chance to be misunderstood)

1. Here they come
2. Here they come
3. Like children with pins
4. And soldiers with spears

1. They're the big people
2. The brutal people
3. The tired people
4. The dreambusters

1. They're the talking people full of words
2. Little words
3. Bubble-busting words
4. Sharp little words

1. Words like, "Do as I say, not as I do"
2. "Brush your teeth and polish your shoe"
3. "Go off to war and fight like a man"
4. "Be a good little boy till you're as old as I am"

1. "Be nice and obedient"
2. "And make like a dog"
3. "Love the establishment"
4. "And cut your long hair"

ALL: That's what they say. . .that's how they pray
"let's pop another dream today",
a million bubble-popping times a day.

1. Here they come with signs again
2. The symbols of their age:
3. "I know exactly how you feel, kid,
4. But do exactly as I say."

1. "You simply must get your diploma
2. Why? Because I said so.
3. And I worked hard to put you through
4. The college of my choice."

1. "And I've had more experience than you."
2. In other words, "You're wrong."
3. And if you don't love money,
4. "You're sick kid, sick!"

ALL: That's what they say. . . .

1. They're everywhere
2. Like mice
3. Or cheese
4. Or bags of fleas

1. They've crawled into every corner
2. Of the school system
3. The political system
4. The church system

1. Don't do this. . .don't do that
2. Don't say what you think. . .don't think what you feel
3. Don't let yourself go. . .don't make a fuss
4. Don't be yourself. . .just be like us

ALL: That's what they say. . . .

1. They are the lovers of yesterday
2. Love your country. . .love your draft
3. Love your ghetto. . .love your city
4. Love your politics, no matter how dirty

1. Love our cars. . .love our clothes
2. Clean your ears. . .blow your nose
3. Love our church. . .and long hairy sermons
4. Love your neighbor. . .like even the Germans

1. We will give you a goal
2. We can shape your soul
3. But he's not the type to have as a friend
4. Would you like your sister married to him?

ALL: That's what they say. . . .

1. Here they come. . .the dreambusters
2. Waving their little flags
3. Wearing the right clothes
4. Hiding their inner feelings

1. Don't be too fat
2. Don't be too skinny
3. Don't be too loud
4. Don't be a ninny

1. *Nixon's their hero now that he's IN
2. King is their saint now that he's dead
3. Don't talk about things you don't understand
4. Just be a good boy and run off to bed

ALL: That's what they say. . . .

* or whoever is in office at the time

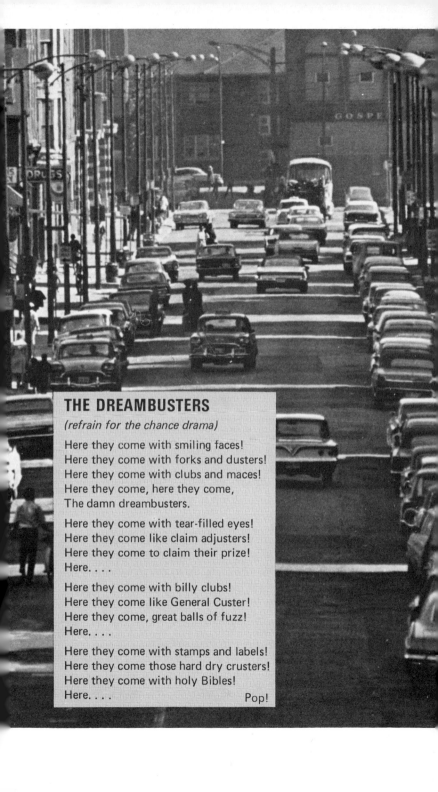

THE DREAMBUSTERS
(refrain for the chance drama)

Here they come with smiling faces!
Here they come with forks and dusters!
Here they come with clubs and maces!
Here they come, here they come,
The damn dreambusters.

Here they come with tear-filled eyes!
Here they come like claim adjusters!
Here they come to claim their prize!
Here. . . .

Here they come with billy clubs!
Here they come like General Custer!
Here they come, great balls of fuzz!
Here. . . .

Here they come with stamps and labels!
Here they come those hard dry crusters!
Here they come with holy Bibles!
Here. . . .   Pop!

A EUCHARISTIC PRAYER : PURPLE PUZZLE STYLE

Celebrant: The Lord be with you.
Response: And with you too.
Celebrant: Open up your hearts.
Response: We open them to the Lord.
Celebrant: Let us give thanks and celebrate.
Response: It is good to do so.

Celebrant: God, Our Father, you created everything.
You make it good and beautiful.
Response: You make bread for our food
and wine for us to celebrate.
Celebrant: You celebrate when you create
and fill the earth with your splendor.
Response: Fill our hearts with the same joy as we
celebrate your resurrection.

Celebrant: Lord Jesus Christ, Our Healer,
you came into our broken world.
Response: You were broken for us
and torn for us to be healed.
Celebrant: You rose from the grave
to unleash new life in the world.
Response: Fill our lives with the same life
as we celebrate your resurrection.

Celebrant: We are bold to ask this of you because, on the
night you were betrayed, you sat with your disciples,
took bread, said a blessing, broke the bread and
gave it to them saying: "Take and eat: This is
my body given for you."
Response: Feed us with your healing body now.

Celebrant: Then you took the cup, said a blessing, and gave it to
your disciples saying: "Drink from this, all of you. This
is the New Covenant in my blood, poured out for you and
for all men for the forgiveness of sins. Each time you do
this, do it in memory of me."
Response: Revive us with your life-giving blood.

Celebrant: Holy Spirit, You bring men together to sing and love and celebrate the Lord.

Response: You are making a new creation from the torn pieces of God's puzzle.

Celebrant: You are inviting us to attend the feast of celebration at the new creation.

Response: Fill our spirits with the same hope of a day when all things will be together. Amen.

FREE AD

(for church bulletins)

Headaches, take Aspirin

Tension, take tranquillisers

Depression, take Vanishing Cream

Boring Church Service, take . . . Off